Archway Publishing books may be ordered through booksellers or by contacting:

Archway Publishing
1663 Liberty Drive
Bloomington, IN 47403
www.archwaypublishing.com
844-669-3957

Because of the dynamic nature of the Internet, any web addresses or links contained in this book may have changed since publication and may no longer be valid. The views expressed in this work are solely those of the author and do not necessarily reflect the views of the publisher, and the publisher hereby disclaims any responsibility for them.

ISBN: 978-1-6657-3017-4 (sc)
ISBN: 978-1-6657-3018-1 (e)

Print information available on the last page.

Archway Publishing rev. date: 02/10/2022

Hunter's Heart
I was Born with a Congenital Heart Defect

Written by Shannon Pierce
Illustrated by Katie Yost

For my brave and beautiful son, Hunter. Let your scar shine!
And with enormous gratitude to Dr. Luis Quinonez and
Dr. John Kheir. Thank you for dedicating your lives' work
to saving tiny hearts like Hunter's.

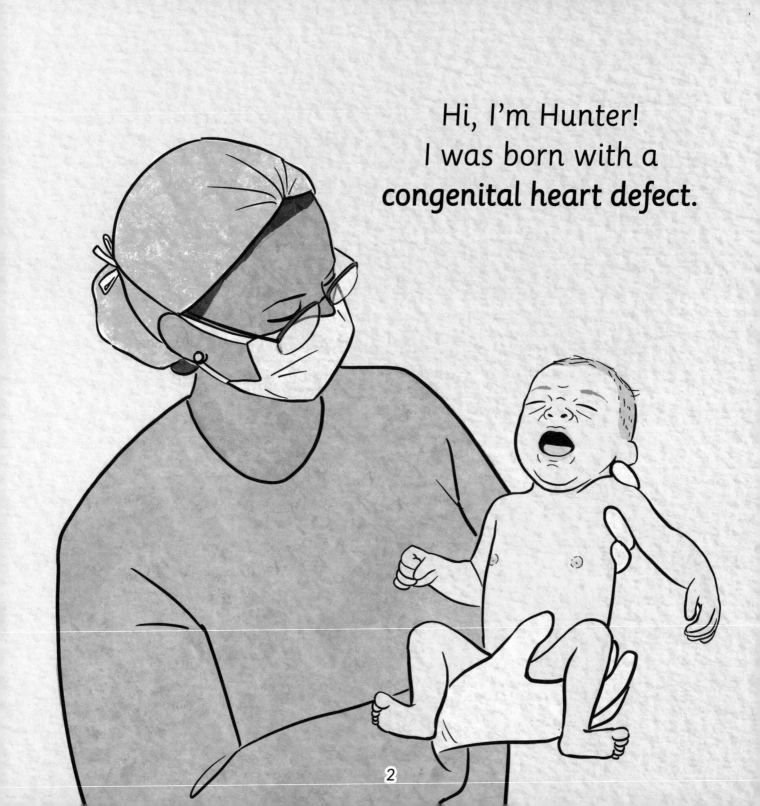

Hi, I'm Hunter!
I was born with a
congenital heart defect.

2

Nobody knew at first
that my heart wasn't perfect.

As a winter storm in Boston raged outside,
doctors and nurses looked me over
at Mommy's bedside.

4

I started turning blue; my oxygen levels were low.
I was fighting my own fight
like the storm blowing the snow.

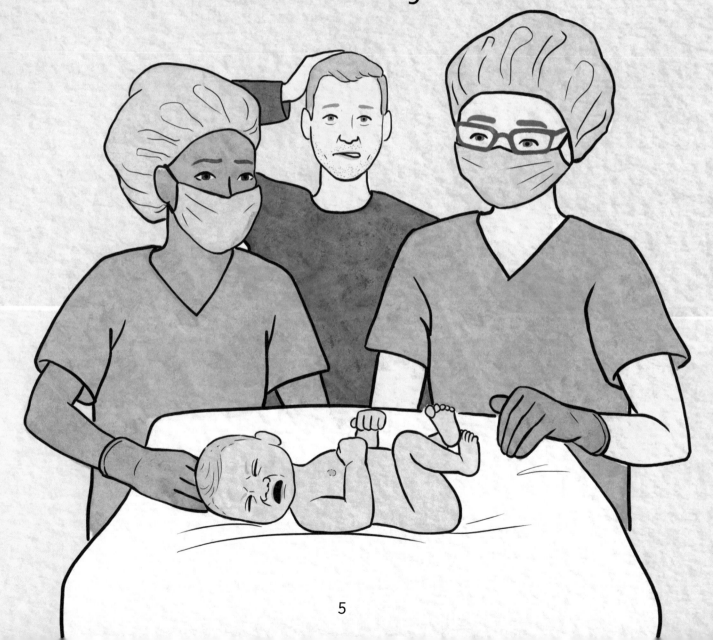

Outside there were no cars on the road
and time stood still;

tests were taken and minds focused, until...

..the doctor said,
"It's Hunter's heart; he's very sick.
He must be seen by a **cardiologist** now – quick!"

Mommy held me close and kissed me softly on the face.
She handed me to the **paramedics**
and gave them their space.

Daddy came in the ambulance
to another hospital down the street,

from Beth Israel to Boston Children's,
where we would meet…

...my cardiologist. She said,
"Hunter is one of the unique babies
who has **TGA**,
or **Transposition of the Great Arteries.**"

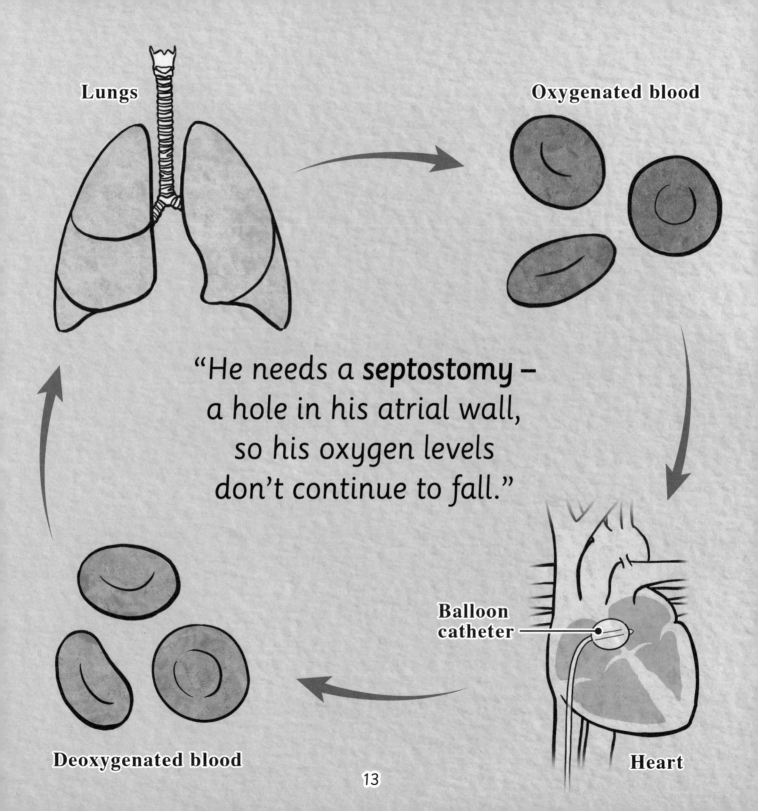

Lungs

Oxygenated blood

"He needs a **septostomy** – a hole in his atrial wall, so his oxygen levels don't continue to fall."

Balloon catheter

Heart

Deoxygenated blood

She explained, "In a **healthy heart**
your aorta connects to the left ventricle part,

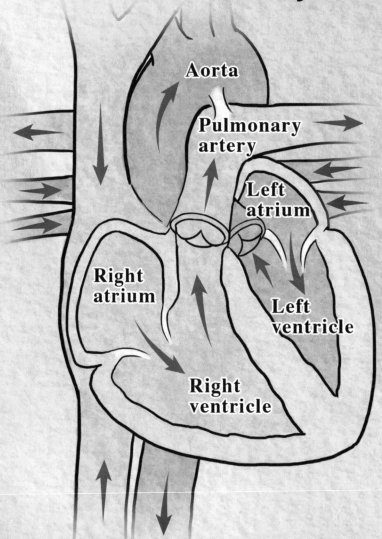

and your right ventricle connects to the
pulmonary artery."

"But with **TGA**, it is all to the contrary.

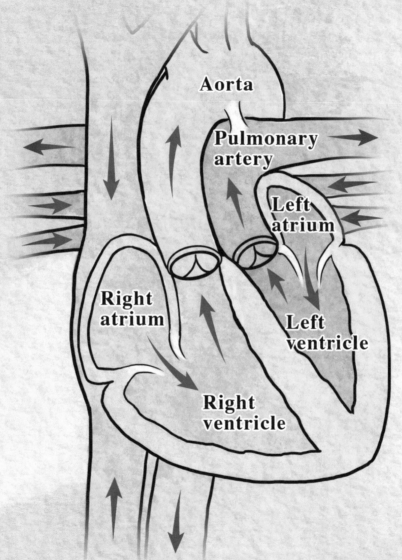

The heart's anatomy is the complete opposite.
Open-heart surgery is the only way to fix it."

The news of my broken heart traveled around the world.
Everyone's love filled my room; around me it swirled.

The next morning was surgery day.
I was five days old.

Nine long, anxiety-filled hours
were about to unfold.

It's time
to trust us.

One by one my surgery team
explained their role
during my **arterial switch** operation
to make my heart whole.

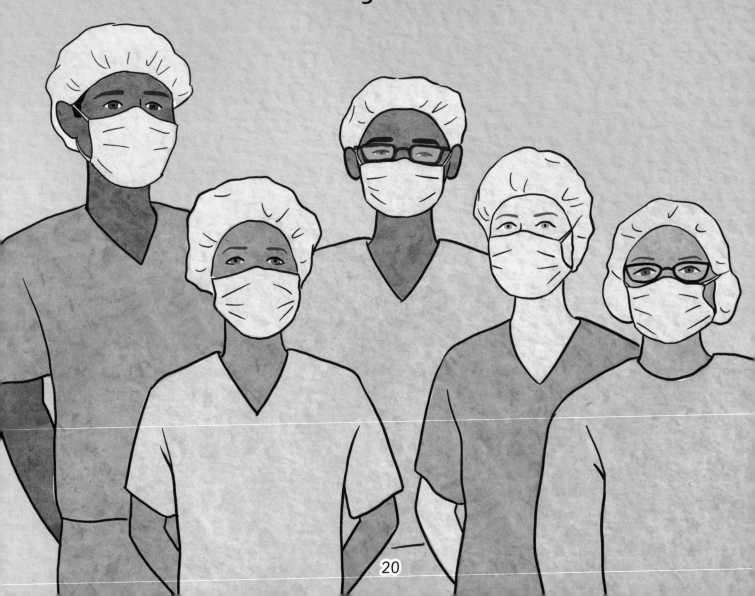

My heart surgeon was especially kind.
Thoughtful, patient – no question did he mind.

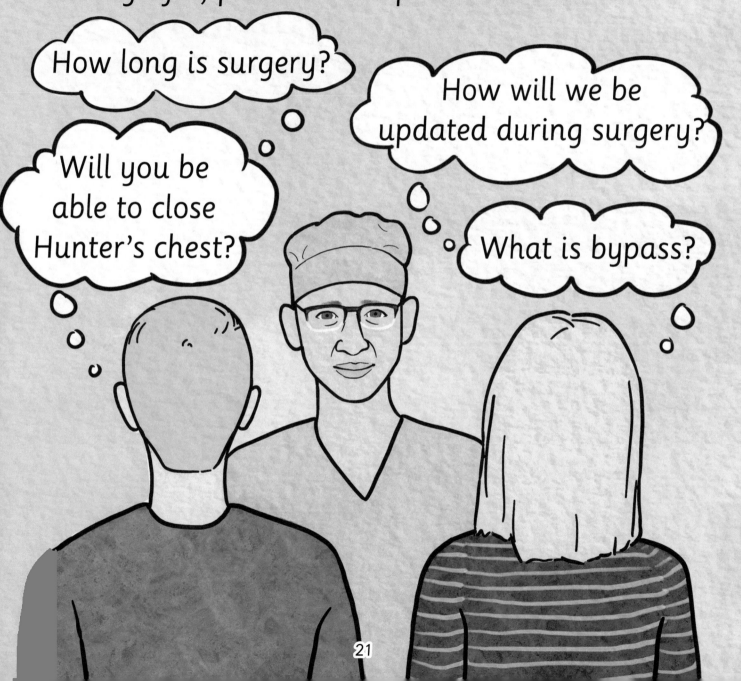

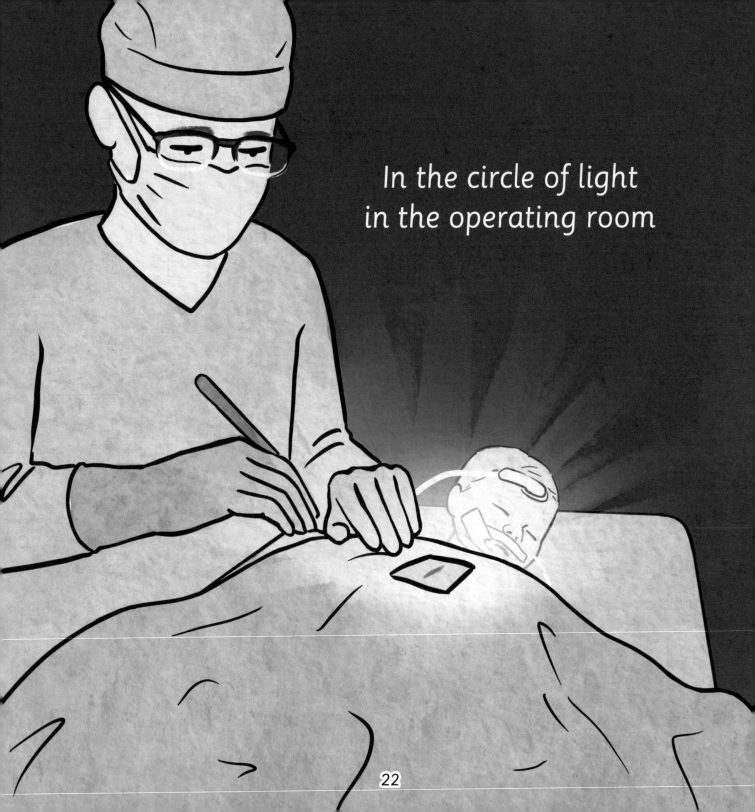

In the circle of light
in the operating room

decades of research
guided hands to avert my doom.

Dr. Vivien Thomas - 1940s

Dr. Alfred Blalock - 1944

Dr. John Lewis - 1952

Dr. John Gibbon - 1953

Dr. Walton Lillehei - 1954

Dr. William Mustard - 1963

Dr. Aldo Castaneda - 1983

One... two... three... four...

the hour hand moved slowly round.

At last! My surgeon appeared smiling:

Success!
Hunter's heart is fixed
and we closed his chest.

"Hunter will heal quickly;
he's a strong little boy."
Mommy and Daddy hugged and
cried tears of gratitude and joy.

"We will listen to him," the doctor continued, "and remove each tube when he's ready."

"Hunter will move
from the **Cardiac ICU**
to the recovery floor
as soon as he's steady."

"The biggest challenge
will be getting Hunter to eat,"
he said.
"Feeding is Hunter's next feat."

Daddy made a chart:
how much "beast milk" could I ingest?!

BEAST MILK ☺

1/11	6PM	45mL
1/11	8:15PM	30mL
1/11	11:00 PM	35 mL
1/12	12:00AM	5mL
1/12	2:50 AM	55mL
1/12	6:30 AM	60mL
1/12	9:30 AM	50 mL

Plan
☑ EKG
☐ labs
☐ CXR

Silly Daddy! Not "beast milk"…
it was milk from Mommy's breast.

It only took eight days –
I was eating like a champ!

I passed the **car seat test**
and we got our discharge stamp.

Finally, we were home as a family of three
figuring out our new normal,
the way it should be.

33

What remains is a **scar**
down the middle of my chest,
a victory sign for kids
who have faced a similar test.

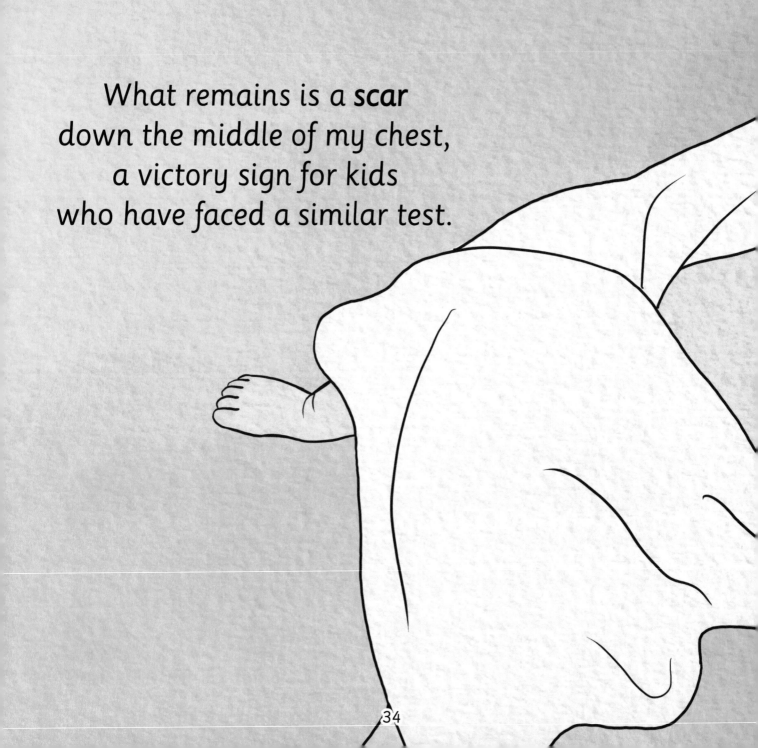

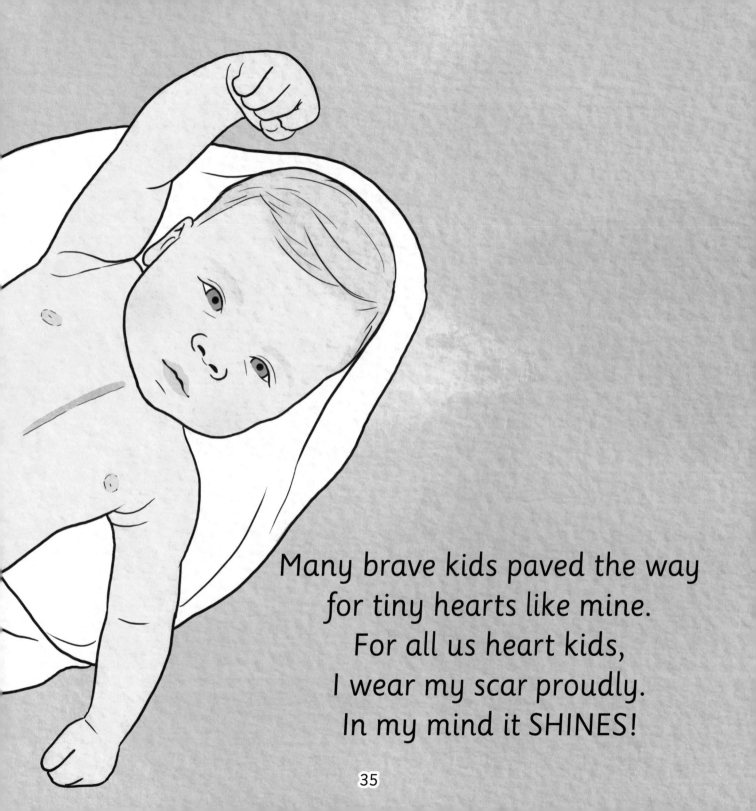

Many brave kids paved the way
for tiny hearts like mine.
For all us heart kids,
I wear my scar proudly.
In my mind it SHINES!

Printed in the United States
by Baker & Taylor Publisher Services